TIFFANY RENEE WITHAM

I0149098

Catching

Smoke

POETRY FOR

LOVE, HATE, AND THE BEAUTY

THAT SURROUNDS US

Catching Smoke

A Book of Poetry

By Tiffany Renee Witham
Published By: Tiffany Witham

ISBN-10: 0692092927
ISBN-13: 978-0692092927
LCCN: 2018943469

fb.com/TiffanyReneeWitham
Instagram @catchingsmoketrw

Printed in the USA

Contents

Table Of Contents   3

Introduction   4

Acknowledgments Page   5

Heart of Fire   7

Frozen Heart   31

Mended   51

Sightless   77

About The Author   114

We Love Feedback   115

For all the hearts that have broken because of love

Steep in the pain only for a moment

Then mend your heart

So that you may love again.

This book is dedicated to the women who have always supported my dream of becoming a writer. Without you, I wouldn't be half the woman I am today. Grandma, Mom-Cindy, Karisa, Darlene, Aunt Hanna, Aunt Lisa, and Karen H.

Heart of Fire

Love
Is the color of big blue eyes.
It happens when you haven't even met yet.
It sounds like cooing and lullabies.
It smells like baby lotion and spit up.
Love

Full Bloom

You are my heart beating outside of my body. My greatest achievement on this Earth is you. Every tear, every argument, every one more drink of water before we say goodnight, you were worth it. Let no shadow move in too closely, for I will be your light. I am your Mommy for every part of this life. -For my sons

Treading in Tandem

Please do not make me promises in the early morning light. Promises of every tomorrow, and heart to heart until death do us part. I have stood where we stand now, ready to fall, ready to jump. Too scared to feel, and too happy to see where all of this new emotion will lead us. Please do not hold my hand so tightly, you do not realize you are squeezing my heart. Every step we take in tandem makes me weak, too weak to walk alone. Please do not utter the words if you have no intentions to stay with them. Watch the sunrise with me, only to part ways before sundown. Tread softly, I do not want to hurt any more. -For R.R.

Lusty Love
It smells like sandalwood and aftershave.
It tastes like medium rare filet mignon.
It sounds like racing heartbeats and laughter.
It feels like perfection.
It looks like dreams for a future.
Lusty Love

BDR

Beating little heart
Tiny fingers reaching out
Smile that melts me

L.A.W.

See
His eyes
Sparkling in
The midday sun.
He sees everything
As if it is brand new.
Every day gives way to new
Possibilities that are wild
And never ending! His loyalty
And enthusiasm is very inspiring.
His hugs are the warmest hugs that you
Can imagine. He loves with such
Unimaginable depth,
It almost hurts to feel.
My little boy stole
My heart with his
Very first
Tiny
Breath.

My Grandfather Bill

Missed by so many
You were so loved

Generous provider
Rather fond of big hugs
A strict moral code
Nothing meant more than family
Daddy to Donna always
Friend to confide in
A wonderful man
Teacher of math
Healer of boo-boos and owes
Earnest to a fault
Really stubborn!

Best Dad and Grandpa
I love him so much
Laughter was contagious
Lonely for his daughter
-For A. W. W.

Grandma
Cranky
Without coffee
Must give her attention
Strongest woman I have known
Miss her – For D.E.W.

Mommy's Future

Arms outstretched to find
familiarity where there isn't any.
Their voices are muffled now
Swallowed up with years of silence
And lost hope. Death can steal
So much from those who aren't willing.
A mother's love knows no boundaries
Except the graves cold embrace.
She can't spout words of comfort
Only silence in the serene hill top of
Rose Hills. Tears stain the sun burned face
Of a daughter who longed for nothing more
Then to follow in her mother's footsteps.
Warmth from the summer heat envelops her,
Suffocating her, choking off all her emotion.
Her arms grab at nothing, fill with nothing
And she knows this is all she will ever have.
-For my mother D.M.W.

The Journey

There is an inevitable time where we all must put away our toys and give ourselves over to growing up. And in our quest to be adults we put away silly things like hugs, and kisses, and bedtime stories filled with true love wishes. We forget to say I love you and truly mean it. We leave the nest and pursue our own adventures, forgetting the people who helped us get there along the way. But I never forgot you Mommy. I may have failed to call a time or two, but never once did I fail to remember my love for you. It is because of you that I followed my dreams, your gentle push and simple words of wisdom I will carry with me always. You'll never know how you molded my views and made me grow to admire you. Although you are gone from this world I know wherever I am you will still fallow. As the days move fast I will not forget the way you made me laugh, I often find myself laughing as tears too soon do fallow. Today was a tough day, I know more are sure to come, but I will bask in my memories of you and I. I will recall the love you shared with me, I will revel in the love I saw in you and Bill, and I will know that although we are apart I will see your face again sometime.

-For H.G.

Baby Talk

I keep having this recurring dream where I wake up and I'm about eight months pregnant. I'm delighted at the site of my full belly. I roll out of bed and walk down the stairs, then I see it, this painting hanging on our wall. I'm captivated by this painting. I can't take my eyes off of it. It's a woman staring back at me, tears are stained on her face, the look of agony and loss evident on her face. I travel past her face to the place where her heart should be and I see an empty black hole, blood cascading from the gaping wound. Her large stomach reaches up to the place where her heart used to be. My eyes flow past the swollen belly to the dripping blood beneath. Tiny fingers reaching out from underneath her nightgown cause my breath to quicken. In its tiny grip the heart of its mother, slowly dripping on the floor. I feel a sharp pain in my side and I drop my gaze from the painting to the floor only to see I'm standing in my own blood, and the painting is really a reflection of me.

Mother
Who loves
To the depths
Of her very soul
Broken

Cosmos

I sought to find a shooting star, I lay and stared the whole night through. I sought to find a place amongst the cosmos, the truth to all the universe's secrets. I lay amongst the tall tall weeds, and lazily picked at the fallen leaves. Too soon Fall had reached her hands out to change the colors all around me. I let the chill of the late-night breeze wash over me, leaving her goose bumps to cover me. I closed my eyes and inhaled lightly, the smells of my childhood invading me. I drifted to dreams in the chill of that night, dreams filled with your hand softly placed in mine. Dreams of a sunset stroll along the beach, walking the line of young love. I sought to catch a falling star, to show the way beyond love's reckless desire. I sought to find a place where the universe wasn't blind to dreaming. I opened my eyes and your hand caressed mine, delicately watching the stars align. When I wake I wonder if you'll ever be mine.

Clarity in silence

In the silence of early morning I can hear your tiny breaths. For someone so tiny you move around so recklessly. I cannot help but watch as you snuggle your blanket close. You toss off all your covers to wiggle and stretch your toes. With your little fingers twitching you move them in real close, tickle them across your brow then leave them dangled across your nose. Even after a year you still sleep the way you did in my belly, with your legs tucked up underneath you and your bottom high up in the air. It's moments like these, these tiny little treasures, that I breathe a sigh of relief and marvel that I made you. Every milestone I've witnessed, every small little thing, and I will spend my lifetime in awe of your precious little journey.

-For L.A.W.

Exploration

Kiss
Her lips
Soft and warm
In the chill of
A car hiding in
The lamp light under the
Rain, her scent intoxicates
Filling you up with loyalty,
But alas, you will betray her heart,
You will carry her pain throughout all time.
Thunder claps above the car causing
Your hearts to pitter patter in
Your chests. She smiles, you break
Down, there is no path to
Follow only lust,
Only passion
Her lips are
Warm to
Kiss.
For M. T. R.

The Poison of Young Love

Place
Me in
Your grave to
Show me living.
Kiss me with frozen
Lips that breathe cold death in-
To my corpse and melt the heart
You keep breaking, while I love you
Spews from your dirty mouth. How do you
Kill me with a kiss and wake me with a
Bye? How will I know truth in your love?
Will I keep pining always? I
Was put inside your secret
Garden, the orchid in
Your thorny roses,
Wilting in your
Absence. I'll
Die In
Vain.

Irony

Perhaps you're better as a mirage. Maybe our time together was only a glimpse because that's all it was supposed to be. Perhaps all the dreams we planned on living were meant to be dreamt with someone else. Time changes people, or so they say, you probably wouldn't love who I became anyway. Except my heart's devotion is still with you. You told my cousin you were only a diversion, time would change the way I felt. Time has passed, two years in fact, and still I think of you on your birthday. I may never see you again and the irony is, the fact that I let you go, and I have yet to let go of you. *-For E.R.*

A Prisoner of Circumstance

I can't make you real, anymore then you can make me feel what you want me to. The words you spoke, how quickly they tore my world apart. Vaguely I see truth filtered in your glossy eyes. Who put that pain there? Was it me, was it her? How did time factor into all of this? I can't hold still the heart beats that flutter when you are near. You're in too deep, you could destroy everything with your velvet voice, your secrets, your ability to lie. I've always been good at reading between the lines, but what if this time I put all that aside, wished to find truth where there never was any before? I can't make you real, any more then you can make me fix your problems. I've shown my hand far too soon, you hold all the cards that can leave me unglued. Like a child let loose in a candy store, you savor every part of me. I shiver in your not so subtle gaze, taking me prisoner before your hands can touch my face. Every warning sign goes off around me, as you gently lay your hands around me. I can't make you real, any more than I can stop the way I already feel.

Troubled

Talking to herself she
Rambles on about the time
Of love and how
Unyielding it was to her will.
Babbling on and on about
Lovers whose beds she'd
Eagerly chased down forever, always
Doubled over every morning after.

October Love

Maybe, maybe it was the way you looked at me with the confidence of a nervous child. You were holding my hands, but my heart was beating somewhere in my stomach. My eyes glazed over the passersby, attempting to try and talk to any one so that I wouldn't have to make a connection with you. The bell to my salvation rang, and quickly your hands did slip from mine. Too soon did your lips push deep into me, my teeth puncturing the softness of your mouth. The taste of your tongue against mine and just as quickly as the beautiful moment had began it was over. I watched you walk away, not knowing what the lunch bell would bring. Bright lights of the stage reflected my glee, it was all I could do to keep the memorized lines straight between the thoughts of you and me. So many possibilities brought with the ring of the wind in our ears standing too close under a shady Fall tree. Your hands were in places no one had ever been, and it was the most thrilling moment of my young life. I thought of you in every second after that. The phone would ring and my heart would flip flop until I heard your voice on the other end. And just as quickly as the words I love you fell from your soft lips, the sting of April's chilly air hit my tear stained cheeks, and I saw you walk away from me. Perhaps it was the memories of locker makeouts and fights over why you didn't really love me, that brought me to my feet. But in the ink blue sky line of the 5 am sunrise, I walked away from you. No tears to cry, only a shower to wipe away the last of you, and in a single moment the years of loving you were washed and floating down the drain. My strength came back to me and I was able to love again. It was you who shaped the loves of my future, the way I held them, caressed them, and loved them. You who took pieces of me with you that I will never get back, and no matter how good or bad the time was between us, I will never forget the way you loved me. *-For A.P.*

Little Kitty

Tiny ball of fluff
You would wait by the door
Meowed for some bacon
Snuggled up on the floor
Too soon you left us
Still hear you chasing toys
My first fur baby
I love you little Desi
– For Desdemona

Tough Times Get Tougher

When the baby cries, when the toddler screams,
Remember that you still love me.
When I'm being hot headed, and you feel the pull to leave,
Remember that we are a family.
When everything is going wrong, and you want to throw things,
Remember we're in this together.
Do not ever think that I don't love you. -For R. R.

Frozen Heart

Hate

Is the color of bright red coals in a fire pit.
It happens when you see your ex with his new flame.
It sounds like her high pitched giggles.
It smells like cheap perfume and stale cigarettes.
Hate

Cutting Ties
They found a note in her pocket
She shared some pretty dark secrets
No one knew she was cutting away the pain
We never saw all she hid away

She shared some pretty dark secrets
There was abuse and betrayal
We never saw all she hid away
He'd shut the door and she'd fade a little

There was abuse and betrayal
We didn't see the signs
He'd shut the door and she'd fade a little
Did no one see, he showed up at her funeral!

So much potential swallowed up by grief
No one knew she was cutting away the pain
Her mother's tears will never stop
They found a note in her pocket.

Break From Power

I've got the power to make you writhe in pain, make you wish you'd never met me. I've got the power to make you fall down to your knees and forget the terror when you first realize you bleed. My arms around your waist, my teeth fastened to your heart, one tug and I'll make you fall apart. Thus the spider devours its prey. I've got the power to make you wish you were dead. My hands are nail deep in your brain, but he's had my heart since we were just children. I'm already broken, you can never fix me, all this power to make you loathe me, but you'll never hate me as much as I hate myself.

Empty Home, Full Bed

You seek from her only what you want, not all that she can give you. The life, the home, the family, all things you already have, with no intimacy. You chase down the ecstasy that comes with the first kiss, the first exploration, the unveiled trust between you two. When you wake you'll go back to her. Hold your family close. Pretend that home is where the heart is, ignoring the bulge in your pants. You can utter the most eloquent words while you whisper forever in her ear, but the monster thrives on your beastly ways. In the evening you'll be back at it again, chasing down the thrill that comes from your lover's lips. You seek in her a place of refuge, a place to lay your truths and not hide what you want. But you do not see the destruction your sleeping around will cause. In the morning when you leave, when you go back to your family, you destroy a piece of her, and piece by piece she'll be swallowed whole, lost in the perplexity that is not your love.

Wash
Your hands
Clean of filth
Keep them secured
Holding on
To your
Heart.

Filled with Venom

You have no value
Your body is your only virtue
Your tongue laps up the words that choke you

Eyes see only shallow
Hands touch only skin deep
You have no value

Ears hear lies of tomorrow
Breast heed ecstasies warnings
Your tongue laps up the words that choke you

In your nose the powder
In your veins the power
You have no value

The blade shines bright in the flickering light
Can you slice it through deep enough?
Your tongue laps up the words that choke you

Drips of crimson through each room
Is it easy enough to find you?
You have no value

Your tongue laps up the words that choke you

He Erased Her

What replaces purity stolen? Within four walls she screams for help, she is forced to be beneath him. On top, the world must seem grand, the smile on his face, they must go hand in hand. Tracing each vulgar word with his tongue, she lashes out, but he has the gun. In each rhythmic motion he pushes a little deeper into her sanity, tearing away at her maturity. Only fifteen, life is still new, dolls aren't even dusty on the shelf. Waiting for his arrival, vomit in her throat, she'll erase any sign of being a doll on his shelf. Is she a picture for men to look at? She weeps in the fetal position. A replacement to her innocents, the shell of a woman she was becoming. Among the broken heart she holds, there is no peace, no sanctuary for her to go. Day by day she pieces together the shattered image she once held. Newly constructed to tell each man to go to hell. She forces a smile to shield her pain, never fully grasping there could have been an end. Recalling the bathtub, she's steeped in blood, a baby herself, she'll never have one. Erasing the woman to become a man, he'll never know the personal hell he put her in. There is no answer to fully qualify a correct remark. She identifies with nothing, so she becomes nothing. He erased her.

Just Words

She'll carry your words with her daily. They will float down on her in the middle of a sunny picnic lunch. They will follow her to study hall, and smack her when she sits down alone on the bus. She will cover herself in the sheets of her bed wishing for sleep to rescue her from the words you put in her head. Mornings will bring only clouds of darkness and the lights in the bathroom will only highlight the cuts that continue to glow blue-black-red. The makeup she wears doesn't cover up the pain, it only masks the vacant shell you left behind. Did you know your words would lash at her heart daily? When you said you never loved her, did you know she trusted only you? When you said you used her up and now she's got nothing left to give you, did you know you were her only one? Did you ever stop to think how your poison would affect her? She'll carry your words with her daily, and they will slowly kill her.

Cheat

Give me peace from my mind's constant wondering. I see her face, your face, her lips, your legs entwined. I see the bodies, your bodies pressed together. All is replaced and I'm left behind. Where was I when your love was so blind? All broken, all lost, give me a shotgun to blow away the pain. I want to feel relief from all the bullshit that remains. It's a nightmare that seems to have no end. I know I can find forgiveness. This betrayal is of the worst kind. Taunting me, mocking me, I want to hate you both, but I can't form the words, my hearts uneasy rest. Sleep I yearn for it. Where is our happy family now?

The Death of Buddha de los huevos

In retrospect, oh well it's all in retrospect, that's all life is, moments to look back and see the decisions you made laid out behind you like some screwed up train wreck. Cobalt blue skies marking the moments you fell short of your goals, while watching him spit into your fountain of youth. He said he'd bleed crimson but you missed the part about him being stuck while the past surrounded him. Retrospect, looking back and seeing it all for what it was and not what you wanted it to be, his falsities laid out before you like some trophy. Except this ending has no happiness we do not die and get reborn into fire birds, the eternal phoenix. There is no crystal-clear water for you to swallow down his intentions, for you to feel the pain that engulfs his existence. In the arms of another how can there be pain? Only pleasure, only lust, only longing, only rejuvenation, there is no one to trust when Faith is dead and gone. If you held the gun but he pulled the trigger who's really to blame? You didn't have the strength to walk away, but you sure pushed hard enough. Your love became a broken triangle, a piece always missing from the top. He may have screwed her, but you went through the motions. In retrospect it didn't hurt as bad as it should have, if you had still been in love with him, it probably would have. All we have is time to ponder the things we could not change, and hope to not make the same silly mistakes again. *-For O.A.*

Attack From Within

The image of you watching me in disbelief as I pull your
heart out to watch you bleed,

That is what gives me the strength to feel again.

It was the curve of your mouth as it angled in horror,
too weak to say stop, too choked to breathe, hallow.

Oh, how your hair danced and meshed along your puffy
red cheeks, mating and drowning in pools of crimson
purple, deep. Your hands clawing for salvation and
finding only the white skin of my back.

Layer by layer beneath your nails,

Slowly seeping into your attack.

One beat left and a small spark of hope, you let me in.

Was I all you had hoped?

Jealousy

Just because you can, doesn't mean you should

Envious so you had to take all you could

Always up to stab your friends in the back

Laughing while you hold his heart in your hands

Overwhelming hatred from the look in your eyes

Ugly on the inside but pretty where it counts

Sexy will only get you so far in life

You are the reason girls hate each other

-For B.C.

Being Chased

Help!

Find me!

I am lost!

She will find me!

Tear the cord.

Curse her.

Fall.

SEEING IN THE DARK
TRUTH.
I SEE.
YOU TELL LIES.
YOU DISGUST ME.
I STRIKE YOU.
FALL DOWN.
WHORE.

It is in the way....

It is in the way he kisses her goodnight.

Slowly he'll turn from her bed to turn off the light.

It is in the way he smiles at the kitchen table,

Laughing at his funny pages while he waves goodbye.

It is in the way he watches her walk home from school.

Eyeballing her skirt ride up when she sits on the stool.

It is in the way he pushes his perversion into her sanity

without hesitation, as he takes control of her.

It is in the way he says he loves her body,

hugging her mother as he smiles at her.

It is eternal hatred for a man who never fathered her.

Turnabout is fair play

Piece me together.

Find the piece that fits inside your dreams, that comes out in flows of erotic ecstasy.

Weed through the mixed emotions that I bring to you.

Drown within the tide that covers you whole and breaks you up to me.

Glue each shattered part of yourself to the morality you cling to.

Show me that you'll feel deeper than you imagined.

Piece me together inside your heart, so that I may know your true feelings.

Let me fester in your brain like a bed sore and bleed me out in your summer nose bleed.

Find the one piece of me you can love and exploit it.

Hurry, because you fear I'll do the same to you.

Lover's Game, I've lost

Thoughts are jumbled, heart heavy with discontent. I'm not the kind of girl who waits around to be picked. My confidence is shattered, I'm not who I once was. I swallowed my feelings to keep pace with everyone. In the years since my divorce from truth I still feel shaky in these new shoes. Love isn't simple, not a game I thought I could play, I've been beaten enough times that I learned to walk away. Words familiar yet so distant tread across my brain, if I never loved him why would I stay? My pitfalls are plenty and I probably don't deserve him. The strength of my Mother's come smacking into view, "he's a fool if he's willing to lose you." Torn by strength and emotion, I hurt far more than he'll comprehend. This game, this game of love, that lovers do, I'm no good at competing, I deserve to know truth. I stood with answers in life's beautiful bouquet while I watched each petal wilt and rot away. He never asked the questions and I never spoke the truth. We witnessed years deprecate between us, all a blur, all for not.

Lost
My heart
To your cruelty
Cut away the pain
Love

Mended

Forgiveness

It smells like a winter snow storm after a warm Fall day.
It tastes like hot chocolate on a balcony all alone.
It sounds like the wind blowing leaves off the trees.
It feels like a heated blanket keeping you warm at night.
It looks like freedom.
Forgiveness

Stubborn like your Mother

Time will never change the way I love you
Even though you push me to my greatest limits
Even when you're screaming at the top of your lungs
I will hug you, and kiss you, and it will all be alright
Even when you're slamming doors and cursing my name
Even though you think you're older then you truly are
Time will only show me how you used to fit snugly in my arms
~For L.A.W.

Sisterhood
Bratty kid sister
I was always in the way
Stole the attention
So she chewed my Barbie's shoes
Dropped a golf ball on her face

SIBLING RIVALRY
I STOLE HIS TOY, FUN.
HE LOOKS EVERYWHERE FOR IT.
I START TO FEEL BAD.
LITTLE BROTHER, HERE IT IS!
WE PLAY TOGETHER, HAPPY.

Walls Come Tumbling Down
Opened up for everyone to see, one by one they all come in, examining me. They point to their charts, they speak in different tongues, and their words splinter in my ears. It's just a small incision, it's minimally invasive, take out the sorrow replace it with love. Questions go unanswered, swallow another pill, make believe it's not like you're treading through mud uphill. Opened up to darkness, let the lights go out ahead, no one comprehends the broken chess game going on inside my head. Knight falls, Queen advances, Rook takes off her head. The King forfeits his crown and buries her deep in the ground. That part of me is dead, flowed out of me in streams of crimson. Opened up for the whole world to see, look closely but do you really see me? Invaded by darkness, taken over by grief, I pull myself up, claw through the dirt, begin again. This is *me* world, open wide.

Wading in the water

How heavy is the weight of the squandered words we wasted in our youth? We tossed around love like it held meaning in the hollow of our shallow mouths. Too deep to reach the bottom too far out to swim back, we wadded in emotional tide pools for the rescuer that would never come back. All the travels we've been on, every road we've limped back through, it all leads back, back to the same stale point of view. In the absence of fertility the messages never displayed, we reach into our bags and pull the pin from the emotional hand grenade. Words spew from us, vomiting on those who care, those who showed up for the torment only to be given the acidic bluntness of our own tired views. How expectant we are that they'll show up another day, always waiting for the moment when they'll make it all okay. In the graveyard of our solitude we blame everyone but ourselves for the loneliness we've endured. Did they not speak to us of compassion, of selfless acts, did we not reach back and slap the hand that fed us with only love and kindness? The word love comes back into focus, but we dare not fix our gaze, or hold out a hand to grasp it. For what do we know of love? Only bottomless tide pools to wade through, only walls too high to climb over, only words spoken in the dark so they can reach in and take all of you. How heavy is the heart that has never known love and kept it?

Out of All My Loves

I love chapped lips with newly applied mint chapstick.

I love the smell of October in Santa Fe Springs.

I love the feeling of freshly washed cotton sheets.

I love feeling cozy under two comforters in winter.

I love how my eyes shimmer in the sunlight.

I love my Grandma's hands.

I love the smell of ground roasted coffee.

I love the way rose petals smell and feel upon my face.

I love the way summer heat burns in Utah.

I love to hear the words, I love you, when it's true.

I love butter on warm cinnamon rolls.

I love all the things I can, but I loved you most.

Wilting/Waiting

I am the tear you weep into your pillow at night. I am the cracked smile you give to people you will never love. I am the lie you spout out to the lover still awaiting your climax. I am the words I will love you someday. I am the pain you feel in your bones when the cold of winter sets in. I am the sweat you wipe from your clammy flesh well after midnight. I am the faith in your grasp, pulsating within your veins. I am the forgiveness you want to attain freedom. I am the happiness you have, because I am love.

The Role Model

I waited my whole life for you to be a part of it. I waited for you to show up at my mother's funeral, I waited for you to come get me at my grandparents' house. I waited to hear that you wanted me, for you to show up. Words are only words right, actions speak louder? But even then, the words were never spoken. When given the chance to tell me anything, you choked on your regret, on your anger, on your faults. You couldn't even say you were sorry. I look at my son, my beating heart outside of my body and nothing could sway me from him. No liquor, no drug, no person, no regret because I'm his mommy. I am his person, the one he'll run to before anyone else. I couldn't abandon him any more than I could the breath in my lungs. Yet you were there, there for other people's kids, you cheered them on, gave them pep talks, listened to their troubles. How sad that my son never knew you, will never call you Grandpa, because you earn that title, just like Daddy. Any man can be a father but it takes a Dad to raise a child. To be gifted the title of grandfather, no greater joy, but that was not you. People say you shouldn't speak ill of the dead but how I can speak well of you? How can I spin the truth in a way that doesn't look bad on you? I waited, waited my whole life to truly matter to you, but I didn't. Your last words to me were angry, your last chance to ask for forgiveness, to say I'm sorry. You let those words die with you and although I forgave you a long time ago, I still hoped there was a better man in you.

-For R.A

For Name's Sake

What would your legacy be, if you hadn't let her ruin everything? Would you know the difference in each of your children's footsteps, or the gentle laughter of your grandchildren? What would have changed if you had sobered up a few years earlier? How could you leave us with so many unanswered questions, how could you leave with her in charge? The legacy you fought for, the pride your Father held, and now it's wasted on someone who sees only dollar signs. She claims grief stricken and broken as she cashes another check. She weeps in self-pity of "how could you be gone?" All the while your children mourn for the man they wanted so desperately to know. Every milestone shadowed by your absence in her ever growing need to have you shackled to her. How many precious moments did she rob you of? What would your legacy be if you had stopped to think instead of following her lead? How different does she look now that you know the truth? Does it change the way you thought you lived, the man you thought you were? What's left of your family legacy, will remain lost with you. *-For W.T.W.*

Bittersweet

Listening to my heartbeat, the heart that once beat only for you, the words of karmic justice come sweeping into view.

> *With comedic offering you steady yourself for some sort of dramatic reaction.*

I have but little to give.

> *The pain subsided long ago, and hindsight truly is 20/20.*

If you were really meant for me, every hiccup, every miss spoken word, would have ended with hugs instead of tears.

> *The years blended themselves, morphing into what was supposed to be an epic love, but it was not and we're both better for it.*

So, the karma is bittersweet because I truly did, only want to see you happy. -For O.A.

Aspirations of the future

As a little girl I dreamed of someone perfect for me.

Someone who would get me in a way that even I did not understand.

I wanted someone to love me so deeply it hurt to be away from me.

I realize now that I never knew what love meant until he held me.

I never knew what forever meant until he showed me.

As a little girl I dreamed of perfection and with him I know truth, I have no fear of what is going on beyond his words because his actions show me daily.

I just wish I knew how to love myself the way he does. -For W.T.W.

Spoken confessions don't mean much to the deaf

Scratched knees and bleeding palms, I wear the marks oh so easily, but no one sees me. I am not innocent, I did some terrible things, he hurt me yes, but no one saw what I did to him. He took it all on the chin and let me walk away clean, let me take the victim stance while he took all the beatings. It isn't fair, how hard we pushed before we cracked. Love wasn't enough to make it more than best friends. Somehow, we lost our way, quickly dissolving beneath our heavy laid plans to make it all better someday. But someday never came and we held on for far too long. It got to a point where I didn't recognize me, and he didn't care to look. I still see him, everywhere I turn, his face laughing at the joke I'm about to say, but nothing comes out, and he isn't there. Silence in awkward hours, emails quickly jotted down to record the moments we missed and how it could have involved one another. But he went his way and I was forced to go mine, so seldom the two will ever intertwine. I got off track I wanted to confess my sins, I did some awful things and I wonder if I'll ever make amends. Crawling forward piece by piece, I'll put myself back into one place, but I'll never be fully whole again.

Emotional Breaks

Emotional block, I'm too emotional anyway.

The tears they flow, wish they'd flow back into you.

I could kiss him, or him, or her, and they'd never really know me.

Hearts racing, skipping beats, feel the pressure of my love making you weak?

Supple breasts with young blood flowing through them, suckle one and be forgotten.

Starvation clinging to the walls of my stomach, cannot eat what does not fuel me.

Passion dwindling, everything aching, put a gun or a pillow to my face today.

Answers streamline their way to me, through me, above me.

Pushing, pulling, breaking apart everything I used to know.

Leaving me, leaving me empty, how can I be full when you hold my soul?

I tripped today, tripped over myself, my love for you.

For one brief moment I forgot about her lips, your arms, her breasts, your mouth.

The clock whispered back to me in green energy 9:15.

Your sheets smelled of us, your cold, your everything.

I want that again. To feel the way I did when nothing was out of sorts.

To feel the way we did when you loved me and could think of no one else.

When I loved you, and I too could think of no one else.

Losing Love

In a room filled with loud music and missing text books you found me. Of all the girls who clung to you, you watched only me. In you I had entered the depths such as no one had before. In me you had sparked a flame that soon burned into a fire. I had never longed for forever until it spilled so beautifully from your lips. Some say I am a poet, but I am just a woman with words to solidify feeling, my feelings. You were just a man who chose to feel and not think. You blurted out words for me to feel your love as I feel hers. The man who led me to her grave under a shower of metallic rain drops and asked for her permission, I recall you wanted nothing but the best. You so kindly offered up your life in return for my happiness. I did not dream your claim that you'd die for me as a fact. Everything is so poetic, so lonely, so wonderful, for you'd drop everything for me. If I left you, you'd leave yourself. If I loved you, you'd love forever. These are not words I took lightly, these are feelings, your poetic feelings. The feelings of a man who had found real love at long last. We shared the same fears, same doubts, there was once something so enjoyable about mine, don't you remember? As a woman I have breasts and a body to keep you warm, keep you satisfied, but you had quoted it was only the heat my words produced that could keep you warm at night. Now it is I who calls out your name and dares to ask for you to answer back. It is I who is losing control without you and is begging for you to help because I ache. We once found each other afraid and willing to find all our answers together. Years it has been since we claimed all our feelings, all our fears. We just assumed, left unspoken, they would resonate through our tears. Now I wake afraid of you swinging that hammer down on me, attempting to release all the love and promises I claimed for you to find in me. I am just a beacon, full of emotion, the depths of which you once swam in. I would love never to see her without you, to feel your palm pressed to mine, your tears echoing mine, but only if you are happy. Only if you find in me what you once found in a room full of people and loud music. Find in me love, for I do and want to love you forever.

Time Traveler

Feeling the slap of his departure
Over and over again as all her
Regrets settle in.
Given the opportunity she toys with
Idealistic love notes and words that were
Very rarely spoken.
Envious eyes draw upon her pain
Nestled deep within her breast.
Every beat of her heart tears at the
Sanity she has left.
Stolen were the moments but time is all that's left.

The Wrong Age

Quiet ride home, I've become no more than a chore!

A weekend to keep close but left so quickly.

I'll never be the correct age.

It's not the way you love me, it's the way you don't.

A common everyday occurrence
I am the fallen tear you
wipe so gently from your
cheek, ever so quiet in the
still of your melancholy, I am
resting. Can you feel me?
do you know how soft my
shell is, and how heavy the
weight of your words are?
I float in to your subconscious,
tickling your fantasies, and in the
rise of the sun I am but a
memory. A passing glance, the sound
of your voice across the hall
you are my freedom, you are my
downfall.
Every breath you take, a piece of
me evaporates. If you swallowed
I might disappear completely.
I am the fallen tear you wipe
So casually from your cheek.

Daddy's Love

Daddy doesn't love me, not the way he loves our family.

Daddy says he never wanted me.

Daddy thought I'd be an inspiration.

Daddy asked for a son, he is sickened by me.

Daddy shouts at me, I'll never be his everything.

Daddy shouldn't push me, I'll snap beneath his weight.

Daddy won't ever know me.

Daddy plays on all my emotions.

Daddy wouldn't see me if I were gone.

Daddy takes for granted the love I share.

Daddy will never comprehend I'll die for him.

Daddy worships a little boy that's not even his.

Daddy does everything for him.

Daddy hates me.

Daddy won't ever accept me.

Daddy doesn't realize he made me who I am today.

-For M. T. R.

Ode to my step parents

A difficult decision,
Becoming a parent to someone else's child.
Cheered me on at all my high school plays.
Don't forget about me.
Everything wasn't always easy.
Fights about attitude, I'm sorry.
Give you a letter to make it all better.
Hugs weren't something you were used to giving.
I never gave up trying.
Just want to make you both proud of me.
Keep you both so close to my heart.
Loyal to me, just because you love me.
Mom, that's what you are to me.
Need to tell you that more often.
Open up your point of view.
Please always know I love you.
Quit all that fussing at each other.
Respect the family we created.
Stop any doubts you let creep inside your mind.
Tom, you're my Daddy for all time.
Understand that blood doesn't make a family.
Value your opinions of me.
Wouldn't trade you two for anything.
'Xtremely lucky you chose me.
You gave me love.
Zest for life, came from you.
-For Cindy & Tom aka Mom & Dad

R.G. Says

*He chased me for years just to see if I'd love him.
Pretending he was my friend, he took all my secrets
and played with my head. Time after time I'd go to
him, telling him what a fool I'd been. Well he told
me, "I love you, don't you see? I can't be your
friend, unless you'll be with me!" What a fool I'd
been, you had deceived me. Well "no" I said, "I
don't want to be yours. I don't love you that way."
He says, "forget you, you'll end up alone." Well the
chasing stopped and I lost what I thought was a
good friend.*

R.G. Says It Again

"Do you think it's possible to love two people at the
same time? To feel like two completely different
people with each one?" "I do," I said, "I know it, I've
felt it before." You were too busy chasing lust to see
I was in no place to be loved because I didn't love
me. I put my trust in you, laid everything out bare
to you. But I am not what you were chasing. You
wanted the past, to feel something you'd lost.
You've always made me feel everything that comes
from you, comes at a cost. I see the choir boy stuck
at the crossroads, afraid to move forward, afraid of
what your family might think. I never said these
things, I never wanted to hurt you. The words left
unspoken, and I don't think you ever realized all
the emotional hell you put me through.

Holding Grief

If you had never taken that pill
If you had never swallowed that drink
If you had never taken those men home
If you had never shot up that drug
If you had never put that before us
You would have seen them graduate
You would have seen them play
You would have heard their music
You would have held your grandkids
You would have been their mom

Sorry isn't enough
I miss you
Every day I looked for you
The chair was empty
Your books neatly stacked
I am truly sorry
But that will not bring you back

Sightless

Sadness
Is the color of cobalt blue walls.
It happens when the sunrises on bad decisions.
It sounds like running shower water.
It smells like dirty laundry.
Sadness

Reflection

Mother

Who loves

To the depths

Of her very soul,

Broken

Three Year Old Logic
But why mommy, why?
Jump on sofa, climb on desk
'Cuz I am a boy!

The Best Friend
Trustworthy
Honest to a fault
Empathetic to all of those in need

Better person than most
Enormous heart
Sappy in her love life
Tender towards her children

First person I call upon
Reasonable in her advice
Easy going personality
Nurturer by nature
Daughter of God *For D.N.*

SOCIAL TECHNOLOGY
LOW BATTERY, HELP!
WHAT IS THE WIFI PASSWORD?
NO RECEPTION? WHAT?
WHY DID I GET A FEW LIKES?
LOOK AT MY FOOD PICS, YUMMY!

School is in session
Bells are ringing, we must go to class.
Shots are fired, we all hit the mat.
Run to safety, do we know where that is?
Is the shooter that disturbed kid that's sitting next to me?
Stand in line to take orders.
Run for cover with our eyes closed.
Are we safe now?
Do we come out and fight?
The blind lead the blind if we cannot meet eye to eye.
"Guns don't kill people, people kill people,"
But the weapon is up for choice?
Say that to the father who will never hold his son again.
Say that to the mother who grew her daughter in her womb
for 9 months but will never see her graduate.
Say that to the parents who must identify the 15 year old in
the black body bag.
The bells are ringing, and we're all tardy.
We're late to the meeting where we put our children's
safety first.
Wake up, put down your lattes, stop watching that funny cat
meme and listen to the cries.
Listen to the shots being fired right outside your door.
Are you scared now?
You should be.
We all should be.

The Cold Room

Hot, cold, dark, light, turn the flame higher, twist the blade deeper, warm blood, cold air.

The chill reaches her core, what if she doesn't want this life anymore?

Sit, stand, pace, waiting for a positive sign, never want more.

Cross the line between the living and the dead, can't figure out all the symbols running through her head.

Examiners slowly protrude, see nothing, see everything, see darkness in the place where life should be.

Go home, take another pill, take another shot, fill the night with dreams that turn to nightmares, wake to pace the floor again.

Picture perfect smile to fool the world, cross your fingers, cross your legs, there is nothing left to unfurl.

Waiting to breathe, waiting to live, waiting to feel happiness in the place where the Devil dwells.

Idle hands, no work to do, feel the razor's sharp edge as it cuts.

Hot, cold, dark, light, the shadows in the bathroom take flight.

Blood sweeps across your view, the tile reaches up to greet you.

Everything is darker, clearer, more relaxed, you can taste the freedom you've been longing for.

Screams in the absence of your wake, lose consciousness, lose faith.
Let go of all your worldly pain.

Barren

Recklessly she strikes out at those around her. Tormented by the demons who reside inside her, she makes insidious choices. Below the barren making of her heart she bleeds truth, she will only break you. The task is always laid before her. Empty in the place of life.

The rain does fall fast
It seems to shade the world gray
Gray as my evil eye

The orchid blooms
White as snow in the darkness
It haunts the swamp.

Summer burns red
Winter freezes all charcoal
Fall leaves upside down.

Black tulip rise up
There is water to be had
Rest now black tulip.

Rise up from the ash
Open widely to the Sun
Show your true beauty.

Rose with your thick thorns
Wilting in the summer heat
Your scent is not sweet.

Frozen Hell
Purgatory is right beyond
These very walls
Fiends wait to freeze out humanity
Horror or Sublimity
What anguish does our life contain
That we can lose such hope
To see no resolution in awakening
Shut the door, close out the light

In death,
we are not proud.
In death,
there is no status we are to achieve.
In death,
the passed up opportunities plagues the rotting mind.
In death,
we find solitude in our decay.
In death,
we wait for the bliss that we never achieved in life.

Fairy Tales – Not A Fairy Tale Ending

I built a castle out of boxes but no one ever told me that the winds of time would do me in. I thought playtime lasted forever, that you could use your imagination to will things to happen. Disney taught me that one day my prince would come, but they never said he'd need me to rescue him. They never said he'd have a past full of unpleasant things and the wicked witch in his life would never leave. I built a life for myself with pleasant smells and sweet treats, no one ever told me that grass and rose petals don't really make up good tasting things. I thought in make believe all your dreams come true, no one ever told me that all your dreams could be robbed from you. Once I twirled the pretty red bird so hard to free her from her cage, and all I got was paper cuts and wrinkled drawing paper. I caught a glimpse of myself in the mirror that tells no lies and it just stood there staring back at me. I wanted a fairy tale happy ending the one that was always promised to me, no one told me that disease could take all my memories from me. No one ever talks about the heartache that comes from broken homes and miscarriages, or the pain that comes when Prince Charming does nothing but lie and cheat on you. I built a castle full of heartache and regret because no one ever told me that fairy tales are just that, stories to be told to dream of pleasant things.

Alcohol

Potent,
Elixir of truth,
Swallowing him.
How fast
His clothes drop
Because of you.

Sex
Felt
Your hand
In dark places
I wanted more
Lust

A hole in the front door

I've lost all reason when it comes to you. I pour out my heart and you say, "I'll bleed for you." Grand gestures of faith and devotion, everything is all screwed up. A blade to the wrists and you withstand the pain, the tearing of my heart, can you hear me scream in vain? You promised forever, could you take that away? Misunderstandings because we don't communicate, explosive conversations only leading to guilt and more pain. "I'll bleed for you, if it will make you understand." You don't realize the life you're taking in your hands. You talk of love and family as though you'd give it in a heartbeat. While I'm the one standing between you and the quiet. Resting on your shoulders I gently heave with each sobbing breath, how close do we come to cheating our own death? "You'd bleed for me," yes this I'm to understand, but where's my reward, bleedings not so grand. Every fourth week I leave pieces of myself and I don't make grand gestures to have you pull me out of myself. Yes, I'll bleed for you if it will make you see your happiness I put before my longing and I don't take in your seed. Pill by pill I drink them down and wash away the pain. Yes, I bleed for you quite literally, and I don't think you'll ever understand.

-For W.T.W.

Confessions of a Killer

If you looked into my eyes you'd never know it. The innocence inside it must never be shown. I am a murderer.

Spoiled Behavior

I've felt the punishment of your wrath, how deeply it penetrates the skin. You leave me breathless while you ease the dagger in. I never knew the sting of heartbreak until I let you in. Full on bad choices, I promised love until the end. All that love has given me, I find no solace in.

Too much Sex

Weak minded. Dirty whore. Four children to raise and there's no welfare check. Cracker jack house built on quicksand. Her world keeps caving in. Too much sex with too many guys, it is the only way she feels alive. Weak bodied, dirty mother. Four different fathers but there is no love for her. Roach motel, built in the gutter. The world doesn't want her. Too much sex with too many guys, no one stops to see she's dead inside.

From Me . . .

I am weakness, draw only strength from me. I am pain, draw only happiness from me. I am death, draw only life from me. I am evil, draw only holiness from me. I am old, draw only youth from me. I am mortal draw only immortality from me.

Love, Pay Attention
My post was disliked. (looking at phone)
Baby, I miss you so much.
Gotta send this Tweet. (still looking at phone)
Babe, we're over, sorry. *Leaves*
Hmm, go on I'm listening. (Scrolling through memes)

Deflowered

The dirt is piled high, breathing new life
Within it's cold muddy grip, time does seem
To hold its breath. Rain sprinkles the mound of
Dirt to soften its gentle fetus, like
Wings of a newly formed butterfly
The fuzzy steam does sprout from the surface.
At first the Earth holds on too tightly as
If it is not ready to give birth, yet
The tiny green leaves push through to the sky
Rising up, like the hatred in Spawn's eyes.
Out breaks the sun with its ball of bright heat
Ready to cast warmth on its mother Earth.
Sweetness from the nectar of its center
The yellow-green turns to white and unfolds
Seven simple petals full of hope. She
Steps onto the mound of dirt wide eyed and
Hopeful, pulling up the baby from its
Mother's wet cold embrace, all to play a
Simple game, "he loves me, he loves me not."
To the Earth they fall, one by one, alone.

Remember War

Falling bodies reach for their saviors. Flailing through the sky like birds soaring on broken wings. Debris from the crash, falling ashes cover all that's below. Unbelieving eyes watch the horror unfold. Hands cover ears that wish never to be told. A war we never knew was coming. Attack on the innocent, they all gave their lives. One year to recall the horror we all witnessed. New York still in ruins, we unite. Still unable to erase the images but striving for a union we lost long before. It's not over, it's only begun. -*For The U.S.A.*

GOD

To know him is to love him. To stand before him is to worship him. To fall before him is to accept him and to hold him in your heart is to have a life that is worth living. For without him all is lost and we are worthless.

Baptised

The answers are simple.
THe prayer easy to repeat.
The milestone is monumental.
He is watching.
The lord is calling.
The air you breath is sweet.
The water you steep in is hot.
The body is cleansed of sins.
The walk with god is light.

Mexico

The air is steeped in toxic waste. Fumes from too many cars and not enough pollution laws choke out the beauty of the people. Replace the scenery with spoiled goods and dead bodies, the richness of the land, the heritage of a people whose lives had been snuffed out before their time. It's a wondrous place with too much to take it all in.

Utah

Summertime is hot but full of adventure.
Trips to the local Crown Burger for milk shakes.
Random hail storms and riding bicycles, laughing.
Utah was my ideal place as a child.
Winter is long and full of dark places.
Unfamiliar paths to sadness on the icy freeway.
My heart still aches from that broken family.
Medications in place of babies, it hurt to breath.
Utah became a death sentence to me.

Sleeping Beauty

In her eyes the world is splintered, the view from her tower is darker than any could imagine. The pull on her heart weighs deeper than the oceans floor. Those who fall prey to her gaze only find love for her even more.

It's time, time that kills the senses, that finds a way to melt all the emotion down into one stream of consciousness. No one stays in her presence long enough to follow the trail of breadcrumbs that lead to her heart. She's good with the masks, lets everyone see the side they want to believe in. It's been years since anyone has reached into the darkness to pull her out, has no one noticed that she's already drowned? If it could all be fixed with simple phrases, tears shed in and empty room, would anyone try? I answer simply. . . yes.

Rotting Hope

Down here in the cold, in the dank darkness, they'll never look to find me.

Swelling my brain begins to throb.

A dark stain of crimson left upon my upper lobe.

The mark that proves he's been here.

As the days pass my body starts to wither.

I remember the fairy dance above the fire.

Abandon hope here.

Slowly they seep in to my tattered body, eating into what was once me.

Even if they discovered this "victims hide away", they'd never know the piece he stole from me.

My Children

May my children know where I came from.
May they understand who I was.
May they see why I lived the way I did.
May my children keep close my love.
May they cherish the time we had together.
May my children see happiness in life.
May they fall in love often but truly only once.
May they be prosperous with their lives.
May my children grow up to be what they wanted.
May they live in a better world then I did.
May they sleep peacefully, always.

We are Women

We are the future of this world.
We are the voice that cannot be heard.
We are the innocence being sacrificed all over the world.
We are the bearers of your children.
We are the tears that cry on unbandaged wounds.
We are girls.
We are strong.
We are the future of this world.
We shall be heard!
We shall rise above this pain.
We shall rejoice in ourselves and our rights.
We are women, we are.

The moon is glowing
The water is cold as ice

Stars watch envious

Writer's Block

Each page is a day.
Each chapter is a month.
Each book is a year.
Tear away the cover.
It took my lifetime to get
here.

About The Author

Tiffany
Who is loving, stubborn, creative, motherly, and silly
Who is the sister of Karra, Robert, Karisa, Nicole, and Nicholas
Who loves writing, reading, and my children
Who feels love, hurt, and forgiveness
Who needs hugs, love, and encouragement
Who fears death, not being a good mother, and loneliness
Who would like to see Italy, my kids happy, and miracles
Who shares cuddles, advice, and friendship
Who is a mother, a writer, a great daughter
Who is a resident of California
Witham

I started writing around 11 years old, as a way to finally cope with the death of my mother. I quickly found that I could pour out my heart, my feelings, my deepest thoughts onto paper and it healed any hurt I might have been going through. Since that time, I have written hundreds of poems, a lot of short stories and a few plays. It is my hope that my words will help inspire others and help them to heal, the way they healed me to write them.

We Love Feedback

As a writer it's important for me to always strive to learn and keep growing in my skills. I would love any constructive criticism or nice feedback.

Send your feedback to
CatchingSmokeTRW@gmail.com

Please consider leaving a review for this book by visiting:
fb/Tiffanyreneewitham
Instagram @catchingsmoketrw